THE GARDEN
OF
THE FUGITIVES

ASHLEY MACE HAVIRD

Texas Review Press
Huntsville, Texas

FIRST EDITION

Requests for permission to acknowledge material from this work should be sent to:

Permissions
Texas Review Press
English Department
Sam Houston State University
Huntsville, TX 77341-2146

Grateful acknowledgment is due the editors of journals in which many of these poems or versions of them first appeared: *Bayou, Calyx, The Chattahoochee Review, The Cortland Review, First Things, Illuminations, Iris, The Kerf, Louisiana English Journal, New Delta Review, Saranac Review, Shenandoah, Southern Humanities Review, Southern Poetry Review, The Southern Review, Sow's Ear Poetry Review, Tar River Poetry, The Texas Review, Town Creek Poetry, WomenArts Quarterly Journal,* and *Yemassee.*

Some of the poems appeared in the following anthologies: *Knowing Stones: Poems of Exotic Places* (John Gordon Burke, 2000), *The Southern Poetry Anthology, IV: Louisiana* (Texas Review Press, 2011), and *Vision/Verse 2009-2013* (Yellow Flag Press, 2013).

Some of the poems appeared in the chapbooks *Dirt Eaters* (Stepping Stones Press) and *Sleeping with Animals* (Yellow Flag Press).

I wish to thank the Louisiana Division of the Arts and the Shreveport Regional Arts Council for their generous support. I am deeply grateful to the following poets for their encouragement and advice: Scott Brennan, Kwame Dawes, Dave Smith, Karen Swenson, and Eleanor Wilner. Thanks most of all to David Havird for his incisive criticism and unwavering faith in my work.

Cover Design: Nancy Parsons
Author Photograph: David Havird
Apollo and Daphne by Antonia del Pollaiuolo, probably 1470-80. The National Gallery, London.

Library of Congress Control Number: 2014950790

For David and Rachel

CONTENTS

Tree of Knowledge

Every Living Thing

East of Eden

Tree of Knowledge

THE LOST BOYS

They'd played out the name game,
were sick to death of it.
At loose ends, woozy with too much
of the Good Life, while bittersweet
ran through the orchard,
they kept groping for each other's hand.
The choreography was off.

Sober, they got to whittling
fast. Adam was crumbling.
And L.G., with his bloated trigger finger,
was losing his touch.
She'd have to be arrowhead-keen,
else she wouldn't fly.
And she'd have to last—anything's better than clay.

In no time
she had that garden pruned.
She knew where everything was,
from the freshest litter of panther kits
to the sweetest Muscadines.

Ingenious—a Mother to tuck
them in at night, to tell them stories
beginning to end!
No need for growing up. Not ever.

* * *

Who could blame Eve for getting fed up?
Particularly with that infernal puppet-show
they staged day after day:
      Adam, dumb as a post,

the ideal Husband,
wearing out a dog-path,
tailing her—
while L.G., chuckling to himself,
dangled the strings . . .
They thought they held her spellbound.

Boy, were they blind-sided
when she made use of her long-handled loppers
and Adam fell, a wreck of a man, at her feet,
and L.G., unanchored,
floated higher and higher
like a hot-air balloon
and slipped from sight.

CLEANING THE GARAGE

Spun into sunlight, a cat's
cradle caging my bike's
pedal. Black Widow. Not black—
mahogany. A slick bead inlaid
with amber. I reach—
catch myself. Myself

at three, with my smooth
faced uncle. The woodpile behind
my parents' garage, my palm
cradling a jewel with legs.
"He tried to explain," they said.
"You wouldn't hear it."
The slap went on burning.
"How you loved your Uncle Harry."

By ten I had a secret
whose sickness lurked in a game.
"Don't you like this? Doesn't it tickle?"
The poison so numbed me
that when death skittered in
and pinched his heart and left
him a husk on the floor, I felt
nothing at all.

PERSEPHONE'S CROWN

It's for a good cause, they say,
which is enough for me at seven,
a tomboy aiming for the missionary life,
to endure the pink yank of curlers,

caged thorns of crinoline,
white gloves, ankle socks, martyrdom
for the Jaycees' seasonal pageant
in the Raines High School Gymnasium.

The air is stale from last night's game,
the stage gritty beneath mirror-slick Mary Janes
that blister. The grown-ups have sacrificed
my Saturday to this spot-lit night.

My schoolfriends, too public in their mother's lipstick,
are hollow-eyed as the dead big-bowed girls
in our grandmothers' musty albums.
I trust that I am feeding starving children.

Teeth set, back straight, for them,
I remember what the others forget:
to curtsy at the edge of the stage
where white-hot footlights put out our eyes.

I pray to be passed over.
Not me, Lord.
But I am plucked: The Adorable One,
Littlest Christmas Angel.

All eyes follow as a sweating man
takes my cotton hand and draws me center stage

for a kiss and a twenty-dollar savings bond.
Polite applause. I freeze.

Smile, he whispers. *Come on, Sweetheart, smile.*
He shoves the crown down, killing my curls—
tin foil crinkled over cardboard.
It scratches like thorns. And stays put.

FLYING WITH MY FATHER

Copilot at five, control stick at my knees,
I face the leather curve of his seat-back,
his daredevil head of black curls.
"You take over if I fall asleep."
He won't, I know. But what *if*?
How to read the jittery dials, knobs,
fuel gauge fashioned from a bicycle spoke?

Once it escaped—the yellow Piper Cub—
went bouncing across the field left fallow,
off towards Mother's Chevrolet.
(He'd swung the prop
but forgot to chock the wheels.)
He chased it down, leapt in like a cowboy.
Mother's hand clamped into my shoulder.

At take-off she grows small.
Her raised face is a white stone sinking—
baby brother a lump against her chest.

Too loud for talk the bee-swarm engine,
the rattling frame. I stretch my arm,
like his, through the flap into the wind, and wing
over pine wood, tobacco field, dirt road, swamp,
cow pasture, corn rows, milky green pond.
Forgotten the dust of landing, of home,
the arms waiting to embrace us down.

DAPHNE

Three sisters—Daphne in triplicate.

Daddy's Super-8 caught us
racing in frame after fast-fading frame
to clear our orchard of its litter of limbs.
Heavy with emerald branches
ungainly as ball gowns,
our arms do a jittery dance.

Where the bough splinters
the pale wood smells greenly of turpentine.
Mosquitoes shiver in our ears.

* * *

"It's dying from the inside,"
says Mr. Moon
of the pecan that gropes the electrical wires
of three backyards counting mine
in this middle-class suburb.
"Likely it'll bear leaves and nuts, though,
right on to the end."

The tree surgeon points out suckers,
a bark-eating fungus,
the stump of a root hacked years back.
Where the trunk forks, a crater
crawls with grubs and carpenter ants.
"Time to bring it down."

At dusk the branches gather like black lace.

We sisters scrambled up every tree in our orchard.
Now, unsteady, I climb a ladder
amid the late-summer cacophony
of leaf blower, power saw,
car stereo's hammering bass.

I push my face into a smell that mingles rot
with the spongy meat of nuts too green to eat
and the sweaty necks of my sisters.
My feet test each limb
as they did years back the river's edge.
And like the Waccamaw's weedy black water,
dark crawls up between toes,
knits past my ankles,
comforting as socks.
How simply the fibers of skin
unravel, brush other fibers,
begin curing in this tannin,

until my face like polished cypress
blooms skyward.

Breathing at last and fully
with many small green lungs,
I feel the light surround
and I dance with my sisters
in the rolling sun.

WISTERIA

Oozing perfume,
the vine kills exquisitely
in such high style.

The trees have no idea
what's happening to them.

QUEEN FOR A DAY

My Father's Birthmother, a Photograph

My first look at you is blurry,
as his was too, your newborn.
At forty-five, my eyes are farsighted,
astigmatic. You could be my father in drag.
I've had a drink too many.
It's hard to be serious.

With that patent leather bludgeon
of a handbag,
your "We Support Our Boys"
shoulders squared,
you look military,
squinting into the sun
from the back steps of some ordinary
whitewashed house.

Are you a mistress of ceremonies?
Or is that official-looking stole
only a scarf?

All my life you painted frescoes
on sunlit walls of Tuscan villas,
or sang hoarse blues between Dubonnets
in a dark Parisian cellar.

Now truth.
A tolerable marriage.
A spot in the secretarial pool.

Tracked down after all this time,
you should have been alive

at least in some nursing home,
dependent on your legitimate
children and what
grandchildren might show up
with a slice of pound cake
or poly-blend housecoat from Sears.

We could have made you
Queen for a Day.

You must be burning up
in that heavy dress,
those artificial violets clawing
your breastbone,
your scarf sweat-stuck
to the back of your neck.
The sun in your eyes
that look like mine
would give me a blinding headache.

Hold that pose,
that smile.
Don't stop grinning into the camera.
Clench your teeth if you have to
at the man whose shadow hulks
as he mounts the scoured
searing steps.

THE TRIP

1

Mica flecks the asphalt of I-49
southbound to New Orleans—
a bolt of lamé unwinding.
"Highway to Heaven," my husband jokes.
He nearly looks at me.

My first-grade snowflake costume
was a starchy fistful of crinoline—
a thousand hellish straightpins.
I sparkled,
newfallen in the sun.

Anniversary weekend.
February and 80 degrees.
Already clover clots the roadside,
spindly yellow wildflowers,
plastic milkjugs, a dead beaver swelling.

Hawks razor overhead.

2

A convention,
professional window cleaners,
erodes the ambiance of our hotel.
Pressure-washed to the streets,
we comb the Quarter,
buy beads for our daughter—
green and purple balls,
gold babies. An eye out for snatchers,

I cuddle my shoulder bag
like a newborn.

3

Voodoo Museum.
Only ourselves and a hennaed palmist
and a red-eyed blonde with a tangled love line.

20 bucks for a pair of rooms:
20-watt bulbs, incense, dusty cases
of Gris-Gris—dried mice and bats' wings.
For luck in gambling, a raccoon's bony penis.

Hand-carved masks with fat red tongues
glow in the dark above the corner shrine,
candlelit, to Voodoo Queen Marie.
A scattering of plastic flowers,
dollar bills, cigarettes.

Yellowing on one wall, the tale
of the zombie—drugged,
buried alive, dug up, revived.
You have to tell a good story
about life in the afterlife.

4

Spread-eagle on the hotel's smoky
floral bedspread, I hear
through pea-green walls the drunken
palaver of window washers.

From toes gone numb from walking,
pins and needles peck skullward.
They leave only bones,
glittering, anonymous.

Beyond this glassy high-rise hawks,
their talons bloodied,
return to nests impaled by trees
flayed by lightning
or winter's mechanical claw.

WHEN TIME STANDS STILL

Numbed by nights
prolonged by warfare
with once-ally, once-lover,
husband,
my brain's gone static,
my mouth raw as though eaten
by the vinegar of green fruit.

Pollen cakes
the outside world
Miss Havisham yellow.

It is the spring of decay.

Bees gorge on mounds
of rich azaleas.
The blossoms wither quickly
in this heat.

My God, what to do with rooms
voluptuous
with Waterford and sterling,
the Empire dining table,
massive and heavily
scrolled?

The skin of my throat
has aged to crepe,
its color a dusty chartreuse.
I can't stop my hands
from fidgeting with it.
My wrists are corrugated,
unsightly.

Play. Play for me.

The spiders obey,
dancing in their webs.

ACID RAIN

Plastic gazebo atop a wedding-cake,
my mountaintop house, totters.
No stiff couple, glued together.
No walls, either.
Nothing to keep you from falling.
It's an impossible place—

like those rooms impaled
on castle-spires or treetops,
where delinquent princesses
prick themselves into bloody puddles of sleep,
escaping proper marriage work:
spinning straw into nests of gold.

You and I, my lover, come from opposite poles.
Our paths rarely cross.
Today, an intersection:
rain pocking my windshield,
your face melting behind wipers.
I never expect to run into you,

to be shocked into life.
My eyes open into mouths
that haven't eaten in a hundred years.
My hands—the witch behind the scenes
maddens my hands to braid you
into a golden rope, our only way up.

THE LEGEND OF PETIT JEAN

Disguised as a boy, Petit Jean followed her fiancé, an 18ᵗʰ-century French explorer, to the Louisiana Territory. While dying, she revealed herself to him and asked to be buried at the top of what is now known as Petit Jean Mountain, Arkansas.

Dawn peels back one by one
the salty sheets of night.
My heart strikes up, staccato

as the bugs we thought were rain
bulleting our windshield
last night in these Arkansas hills.

Through 20 miles thick as black strap
we hunted groceries for our WPA cabin.
Found a rundown town

with one blinding building. Thank God
for Big Star and Dairyland,
Sunbeam, Peter Pan.

Wheeling back through constellations,
we rolled down our windows: cicadas
and crickets, rhythmic as sex, that strident.

Daybreak: hawks unfold.
They sail from cliff face to cliff face,
as though their valley is a cage.

Unable to hike in this heat wave,
we visit the grave of Petit Jean,
who followed her wandering lover

two centuries ago to these hills.
Green eyes straining towards Orion,
she got lost—a boy in a storm of stars.

On this windy ledge dirt peppers us.
Wrought iron fences off the plot:
pale weeds and plastic roses faded to flesh.

I think of hearts like bats,
their signals lost,
slamming from wall to dark barred wall.

AT STONEWALL

I'm wading through a clearing,
knee-deep in khaki weeds and
coreopsis so yellow my eyes burn.

Over the pines a pair of buzzards
sharpen the groove
of their same circle.

Horseflies—a nimbus—
find my sweaty tangles
trickish as a web.

I kick the head off the blister
of a fire ant mound to open
tunnels like cigarette burns
veining through cemented red clay.

Ants pour out like lava.

I make believe you never
gave in and quit smoking;
and I never began this insect-change,
wormholing into midlife.

I conjure a dim cellar, close dive,

where beneath lazy
ceiling fans, in the haze
of circling smoke, I don't
have to share you.

From low clouds,
the sun's searchlight
sweeps off westward.

Summer's on the rise.
Ride with it.

THE HORSE THAT WAS
STRUCK BY LIGHTNING

The rain was a thousand spurs.
But I was a standing stone in the field.

I know the story of the body,
eyes like fishbowls,
yellowfilmed and flycrawling,
fixed in that wild side-stare of his.
(Freak accident, no one to blame.)

I know about the tractor and the chains,
the four locked hoofs. No choice
but to drag him clear of the pines.

The bonfires. Now there's a story.
You had to burn him three times over
to get down to bones.

* * *

After weeks, my friend,
you bring me to this sun-scorched field
with its riffling wind.

You ford the secret network
of fire ants
to find "what's left of Bay."

Your curiosity is clinical,
a physician's or a cold-eyed child's.
You take for granted my following.

I've known museums
where glass fields the leathered heads
of bog-horses, Neolithic jawbones.

But here I'm out of my element.
This sun goes straight to my head.
Rumors fly:

> *Your guilt is like onion in the grass.*
> *It oils you like good grooming.*

Unmoved in the shade of your wide-brimmed hat
you scuff your steel toe
at this boy's fort of charred logs,
the segments of spine clean enough
to belong to anything—
dog, pig, person.

Your boot scatters dried grass and dirt
over the pods of bone.
Dust rises.

I can't keep my hands away.
In the buried heat of ashes
a shifting, a reviving.

I see the bloom, the luminous worm.
Struck, I turn into stone.

NOVEMBER DUSK

The fog sags like an old fishing net
hung up in the hardwood.
Dusk silts the water brown.
Past season, pondweed rises.
A white shirt in a canoe offshore
gathers soot.

Bonfire,
the only dry thing here,
spawns sparks
like roe gone haywire to surface.
Crevices glow
with the molted snakeskin of ash.

I take up a stick,
spear some flame.
Across my waist drifts a sleeve.
Not his. He's past returning.

The fog melts down.
Tentacles of eelgrass reach.
I hold the stick, the fire,
refuse to drown.

LUNAR ECLIPSE

Hard drinking at the camp house.

Come dusk, we nudge each other
to the pond's edge

where up from the muddy bottom
of twilight
the ruddy moon, a bloated pig,

breaks the choppy surface of the pines.

Netted by mosquitoes,
half-drowned in Cabernet,
woolly-mouthed,

we witness the slow bloodletting.

The moon, diminished,
pale as a communion wafer,
rises.

Our far-gathering shadow,

beastlike, insect-riddled,
swallows it slowly
whole.

VOODOO AUTUMN

No rain for months.
Behind my father's house
the swamp dries to mud,
turtles plod fieldward.
They don't stand a chance.
Buzzards squat in the ruined cypresses.

Night after night brings the lasso of dream,
brown-green as swamp water—your eyes.
Then dawn. Outside my window
the stray redbone hound Dad's taken in
howls for scraps.

I follow the deep-winged arc
of a blue heron, its prehistoric squawk.
Wood ducks scatter, cattails feather.
On a rise, beyond a stand of bamboo,
the husk of a sharecropper's shack
rots into the broom straw.

How to break the night's noose of dream—
your hound's nose sliding under,
flipping me belly-up?
My plates crack. My stump-legs paddle
against the heat.

The fallen chimney's crumbling bricks
mingle with broken mason jars.
Near the rusted pitcher pump to a dried-up well,
I forage in briers and broom
as if to make a nest.

This night, I do the voodoo spell,
turn redbone, split your skull-shell,
jaw you good.
I leave you to the buzzards,
trot home howling.

Every Living Thing

ON CAYMAN BRAC

At first I hardly slept,
the nights were so uncommonly dark,
the lecturing sea so foreign—
a Babel collapsing
through French doors stopped open for the breeze
with ballast beached from the wrecked
Prince Frederick.
I kept mistaking for a storm
a mere fireworks display—heat lightning
to the east
and some token thunder.
Overhead, a smear—the Milky Way.
Never rain.

A cat crept in
those nights and ate craters
in the bread left on the counter.
Paw prints led from the clawed-through
garbage bag drooling mango peels.
I never heard a thing. Odd—
I wasn't sleeping.

But now, after some three nights of study,
I've learned this sea's cacophony of tongues.
And each abrasive whisper translates "sleep."
The deep lungs, moist and fishy,
purr "dream."
This sea—a black narcotic cat—
laps up my breath,
sighs it back.

THE HARVEST

Mid-afternoon, the porch, and a book: *Wild Trees of the Caymans.*
Hooked through the foot, the conch hangs from the railing.
Susan, adrift on her lounge chair, snores.
Crab Bush, Indian Almond, Pepper Cinnamon, Balsam.
It lifts its shell, lets it drop.

At Greenhouse Reef, spawning silted the water.
Conchs: hundreds. We turned them over to the sun.
I plucked from this sea garden of mouths the one
whose fluted edge, butter-yellow, paled
to pink-white translucence, deepened in its throat to rose.

A local told us how to kill it clean—
no gobbets secreted in whorls to stink and draw ants.
A trolling hook filched from her ex's tackle box—
she offered to do the deed. But I'd brought it this far,
off-season, to the house she'd gotten to keep.

Wild Fig, Ironwood, Bitter Plum, Cherry.
The flesh cringed above the stony operculum.
One jab, a second, and the barb twisted through.
Strung up, the snail lengthened, a rope of taffy,
from the swift weight of its shell.

"I can't believe I'm doing this." I'm sweating.
"You wanted it." Divorce has toughened her.
The sea's iris shimmers around patches of Sargassum weed,
brown-red, scabrous. One stalked eye wavers, seems to *see.*
All day, all night, another morning; the shell falls.

Bull Hoof, Plopnut, poison Manchineel.
Etched with pigment from the vivid shell—
mango, papaya, cream—the mantle hangs.

I balance on coral stumps in ripe tidal pools,
release it to the scavengers, those merciful and quick.

PAN'S SHADOW

By dusk you're worn out,
a stinking rag—
what you get for trailing at my heels
like a toddler's blanket
over boneyards of conch and coral:
sun-ripe fish heads, seaweed, crabs.

Some haul.
Pocked chunks of orange Styrofoam.
Green rope knotted into prickly fists.
The head of a doll, its scalp
a peppering of root-holes.
Twenty-seven flip-flops.

No doubloons. No spiny lobster
for our pot. No Glory of the Atlantic
shell to sell for a killing.

We shower.
I mend you back into shape.
We dance around the porch,
drink rum, grill burgers,
have a good time in bed.

Tomorrow, you swear, will be different.
No dragging the beach all day,
netting flotsam, snagging on barbs
of ironshore, wearing thin.

Sure, I say—like I always do—
kicking through battered plastic,
looking for a mate
among all those flip-flops.

ALICE GONE UNDER

Grown up, still clumsy as ever,
she falls overboard
and flails for something to hang onto—
an empty jelly jar,
a soggy two of hearts—
anything to keep afloat
on these swells of giant tears.
Alchemy arrows her body.
She dives past light;
the sea flattens her lungs,
molds them into gills that thrum.
Curious, the viperfish,
its lure's strobing photophore.
Curiouser, the gulping umbrella-mouth of the eel.
Curiouser still, the fangtooth, milky-blind,
jaws of needles incurling.
They make her over, strip hide off muscle,
leave a Visible Woman, slick,
a membraned net of veins.
B-movie tentacles handle her zone to zone—
through Midnight, Abyssal, Hadal,
to fissured crust. Eruptions blow-torch
her bones clear down
onto beds of tube worms and anemones.
Cellophane shrimp and albino crabs
nibble her shreds.
Off with her head!
And giant clams suppurate.

HURRICANE: THE BRAC

The hurricane of '32
laid bare the bones of this ironshore,
a Paleozoic mudpie of coral and mollusk
that shreds your best Nikes
yet preserves a kaleidoscope of flip-flops
borne over—they say—from Jamaica
on bottlegreen waves that sing all day.
Emerald parrots squawk from the sea-grape.

They say a magnetic band
stretches through these islands.
It holds sunset for hours—
wave upon wave of salmon and apricot.

* * *

A find—this grove of coconut palms,
white curl of sand, bleached conchs,
and one salt-rusted truck.
Two young women, coffee-dark,
lock arms around a grandmother
with dragging legs.
They sit her upright in the lip of the sea,
a doll they have to share.
They splash, singing like girls at her feet.

She includes them—no more, no less—
in the sweep of her eyes.

Old one, I've heard stories.
Your soles, in the tease of froth,
might wear a fabric of scars
from your climb to the bluff's caves

across prickly pear and rock
sharp as the teeth of barracuda. . . .

Did, that night, the sea-become-sky
scythe clean from your arms
the one thing you carried?

The backs of my own legs grow heavy on wet sand.
The water—a good ruffled petticoat
ripped and ruined.
I see through her clouds of cataracts
a hurricane of color in the sky,
the flood of magenta
that ebbs at a salt-scorched sea-grape
and a child like a rag doll
snagged by a low branch.

POLLARD'S ROCK

On the south side of the bluff at sundown
we hike to Cayman's shrug-shoulder salute
to Jamaica—a flat-faced boulder
turned festive with flip-flops and sneakers
shunted in by the tide.

We can't avoid accidents—
the way our rubber soles explode
the zebra-snails peppering
fossilized brain coral, star coral,
salt-slicks cratered in this ironshore.
Frigate birds spiral. A sky inking fast

shoos us, stumbling, to bikes
whose baskets brim with orchids
and bromeliads foraged from the mouth of a cave—
cool at noon—
where bats sheared from ceiling to wall,
grazing our ears, nearly,
as though we might scare.

FEEDING WITH THE WHALE SHARKS

"You touch, and they dive to the bottom.
The skin feels like this."
Mario slaps the nonslip gunwale. "Sandpaper.
Now you know, you don't need to touch."

No problem, I think, then plunge,
miles from the Yucatan and its ruined cities,
into a blue sea hazed green with a sort of orange puree.
Ghostlike the sharks (the size of the flimsy boat)
emerge, then ghostlike vanish.
Dominoes, the locals call them.
Submarines, maybe, in domino-camo. . . .
It's harder than I thought, maintaining distance.
One swims towards me, veers past,
remoras clinging to snout, fin, belly.
Its spots spell out a name, a story.
I kick hard to catch up, my hands reach;
I'm driven to read.
The fish, Buick-grille mouth inhaling plankton,
the fish goes about its business.

Perhaps *they* hungered as I do,
the ancient ones of Chauvet, Lascaux, Altamira,
when, submerged in the otherworld of caves,
they felt pulled toward the impossible skin of the stone.
Palms flat, palpating the wall's membrane
for shoulder of bison,
horn of ibex, haunch of cave bear,
they knew what I am only now learning—
the one language, a language of signs,
to tell by hand of this longing.
It took charcoal and hand-bloodying ochre
to midwife deer and mammoth, horse and lion.

And the rock remembered. . . .
Our species—no sooner birthed than left to ourselves,
to our own imaginations.

The fish in my dreams keeps the shape of my hands.
Palms working across gill slits,
down the vast ridged arc of the whale shark's flank,
I feed myself the gritty Braille of the spots.
I sucker on; we circumnavigate the world.
I read to fathom that unbroken life.

RESURRECTION: IVORYBILL

Men drowning dream of flight.
Their bones thin into stems of cattails,
their arms leaf out. Beneath the swamp
water's skin of sky, believing
in the rising of their changed bodies,
they mistake for storm-stripped crowns
the labyrinth of roots. At rest
within the bottomland forests they felled,
they grieve us back into the world.

From the stumps of the Tensas, an uprush—
a dream? Beneath the oar
beat of my wings,
a child, sprawled on a mud flat,
its eyes reflecting my yellow eyes . . .
a dog, its leathered carcass hung
by floodwaters in a scrub oak. North,
towards the smell of swamp decay
and the sharp sweet lily, the rumor of a mate,

I turn the sky aside,
row to this diminished wood.
No red wolf's song, no panther's rip.
Only the rumor—they speak it, the living men
who disguise themselves as trees
and whisper in tree-tongue.
Like the cypresses, they stalk the river.
From them, I have learned to be sly.
Quieter now, I tear into rot-soft Tupelo
and rake the crawling meat.

My shadow falls over water ash
and buttonbush, swamp rose

and lizard's tail, heron and hawk,
the banded water snake,
swarms of frogs small as horseflies,
and men dreaming that I am God.
The rumor of a mate carries me.
The blades of my wings
feather the sky, fan out the sun.

SIDESHOW

What stopped us en route
to Moesgaard Museum's
Amazing Bog Man
was unspectacular—an unearthed grave:
the skeleton of a dog
whose human had taken pains
to fix its limbs as if it slept mid-chase.
The bones were Stone Age bones
from a dolmen that crouched in sea-fog
overlooking Aarhus Bay.
A good dog—surely guard or guide—
to be honored by ceremony.

Grauballe Man was a length of twisted jerky
that took our appetite.
A shock, the tannin-hennaed hair,
clown-grimace, throat-gash,
blood poured into the gullet
of some thirsty god
biding its time in that soggy underworld …

"I miss Hector," our daughter said
of our Lab, back in the States.

* * *

After ten years I'd forgotten
that skeleton already ancient
when Iron Age Grauballe began his curing—
until, still unbalanced from the fall
of New York's towers, I watched on TV
teams searching for anything human.
I focused on the dogs

stumbling atop the debris,
mouthing what we have no stomach for.

On our walks—Hector's and mine—
now gunmetal evenings
smother too early the sun,
I recall survivors' accounts of tidal waves—
of looking up bewildered, mistaking
for a dark arcing cloud
the scythe that was the sea.
I sometimes stop on these walks,
bend my head to his
and whisper for no good reason,
"Good dog." And his breath
is a warm and fishy fog.

Nights, he lays his head
like a twitching brick on our feet,
staying us.

THE DOGS OF ATHENS

At home amid the fallen stones of their temples
and sacred ways, the gods in disguise.
At times, taking notice of our many feet,
they rise from the worn marble,
cool against their bellies. They stretch, yawn,
heal with their tongues one hand or two.
They trot at chosen knees.
Our instinct is to worship. We forget
our guest-hood, forget to keep our distance
from the massive scattered flutings,
chiseled crowns of acanthus, fractured amphorae.
The sharp claps and whistles
of blue-suited guardians keep us at bay.
They wander at will among the toppled columns,
the blood-red poppies and yellow hawkweed of the Acropolis,
dried figs beneath the sprawling tree at Keramikos:
wiry Apollo with his golden beard;
watchful Athena, white breastplate against sleek black;
tall-eared Zeus sitting erect, like a stony sphinx,
wearing on his shepherd's brow the aegis of storm.

LAST JUDGMENT

Megala Meteora, Medieval Fresco

Too-tall thistles nod over the gold bench
where Father and Son must sit, stone-still,
since both are blind, their eyes gouged
down to bone-white sockets. Like children's,
their bare feet dangle, not touching the ground.
Are they deaf as well?—or just bored
by the ruckus going on to one side:
the flushed and red-robed archangel
sealing the fate of the bald and naked
and (insult to injury) peeling Damned?
These wretched ones gaze up, amazed—
past the angel—to the crabs and jellyfish
aswirl in the cosmos, at home with the comets
and stars . . . until their attention turns outward
(the Deity still absorbed in its thoughts)
to the three-legged cat in a black-and-white habit
limping towards us, bleating
in the obsequious high-pitched way of a crone:
Alms? Alms? Alms?

TEMPLE OF THE OLYMPIAN ZEUS

I am a messenger of the world invisible.
I know the way to the garden
beyond the edge of time.
—The hoopoe, Farid ud-Din Attar's *The Conference of Birds*

Still life amid the dusty pulse of Athens:
this massive ruin, post and lintel.
Columns—standing or toppled—
a stacking game abandoned by giants.

At this interstice of marble and cinderblock,
swallows dip and soar like boomerangs.
The gods are playing. A live wind-up toy,
a turtle with painted Egyptian eyes,
rustles through grasses, yellow wildflowers.

Upon a fallen chunk of pillar the hoopoe,
zebra-bird, fans its black-tipped crest
into a Mohawk headdress,
takes me in with one eye,
the Pakistanis peddling sunglasses with the other,

flits past the watch of the guards,
through cloud-gates into a garden.
Spills all into the ear of the sky god,
whose offspring bicker over their turn.
Nearby, rows of postwar apartments age badly.

East of Eden

DAUGHTER, 14, WITH SCISSORS

She still can't use scissors.
She sits on the edge of her bed,
holds out her wrist, blood-beaded,
a bungled bracelet. *I wish I was dead—*
a whisper. Like Andersen's mermaid,
she's bartered away her voice.
Outside in the dusk,
a bedlam of children's noisemakers—
the tide of cicadas in summer's trees.

She can't cut.
While she sang from her heart
to Disney's Little Mermaid,
the canary yellow pair for lefties
mauled paper between serrated teeth.
Wandering free, wish I could be . . .
To spring her from K5,
I sheared 26 pictures from old magazines:
"A—aqueduct" through "Z—zinnia."

She can't cut straight.
I caught her at 10,
remaking a dress and belting
with Britney: *Hit me baby one more time.*
She stabbed the hemline.
At her feet, two ragged arms,
a ripped turtleneck.
Right then I should have scoured
the house for sharp objects.

I curl over her
as though to reclaim her with my body,
reconnect our pulses.

She's *part of that world* of Grimm,
whose spindle will have its way,
the princess seduced to a sleeping wheel.
How to play? She's all thumbs.
Her mouth opens.
The song spins to dust on her lips.

SLEEPING WITH ANIMALS

Our daughter, outlaw at 3, falls
for the dozing lion—
strokes, pecks him with kisses.

No touching—
the guard takes her hand.
She darkens.

A sea teeming with beaked azure dolphins.
A beauty, her eyes hard-drawn
into the shape of lemons.
A gymnast hand-springing
the slope of a bull's back.
A circus! in frescoes.

But the stone—*He wanted a kiss*—
has warmed her blood.
Nothing will calm her
until, tight in her hand,
the gift shop's plastic
Minoan double ax.

We almost missed it—the Phaistos disc,
of clay, small as a saucer,
its spiral of hieroglyphs
evading translation.

A maze of years—
our daughter tumbles out,
15, a cipher in too much mascara,
mad for boys who hunger, who won't take *no*
for an answer—first in line for the pleasure
cruise to the Minotaur.

We excavate to reach sunset's amber,
the sand of Crete,
our child building her labyrinth with beach rocks
pocked like lemons.

DIRT EATERS

Their time near, Delta women with no use
for doctors know to gather dauber nests
for a silty tea to ease their child
into this world. To heal the navel,
a poultice, rust-brown, like raw clay,
that dries brittle—
a shard some keep and treasure.

Summer's end, my daughter leaves home.
As in the weeks before her birth, I clean
everything in sight—even the porch screens
of our century-old house. Unhinged,
hauled outdoors for their first scrub-down
in years, they reveal, clotting the channels
that anchor our floor-to-ceiling louvers,
clumped fingers of mud dauber nests.
I hack at them with a screwdriver.

I never saw the wasps at work,
welding their nests into these grooves,
toting stunned spiders
to cradleboards where larvae hatched and fed.
On hands and knees, I sweep
catacombs crumbling with leggy remains—
wasp or prey?
The nest-dust salts my eyes,
grits my tongue.

DAUGHTER

Swimming underwater,
pushing hard,
lungs burning—
that's what it's like to be
her mother
now she's 18.
In this no-gravity
my bones are bird-bones.

Climbing sunward,
I see the strangest thing.
An inch, half-inch,
before surface, my hands,
out-reaching, mirror themselves.
Each arm sprouts a twin.
And for a split-second
I'm Alice grazing
her looking-glass self.

Breaking through quicksilver,
I choke on air as *she* did
when slickly born.
I turn—just glimpse her,
clear-eyed, seal-sleek,
back-stroking away.
I flutter at the glass.
But the mirror heals,
holds fast.

MANSFIELD BATTLEFIELD

Soggy bag sandwiches, red t-shirts
with mascot eaglets.
We arrive in yellow buses,
my daughter's third-grade class,
for reenactments. No jackets, no umbrellas,
barelegged. No one thought of rain.
Are those guns real?
Amid musket-fire, a woman in wide skirts
churns a black wash pot.

Shell-shocked, my division
locks into a semicircle. Our fake Johnny Reb,
droplets beading his gray wool, drones—
our stomachs growl, we shiver—
drones on and on.
Leaching lead throughout that spring
of 1864, his pewter canteen, cup, spoon.
A bayonet taps out the dead
on the square toe of his wood-pegged boot.
Three thousand here beneath our feet.

Releasing her stranglehold
around my neck, my daughter squirms
down. An eruption: earthworms rise
into the Easter-green grass.
Spellbound, the children dance them flat.
Some fall to their knees.
I grip her crimson collar, hold her back.
Not my child.
I dig my nails into the eagle's eyes.
Not mine. Not yet.

THE FIELD

Remains of a Viking Settlement, North Jutland

Washboard furrows life-masked by sand
for nine hundred years, the field still lies
in wait
for seeding, greening, harvest.

Come night she might sigh in the way of earth:

The first tickling was like love
in a dream, puffs of dusting-powder
that changed into pin-pricks,
into whips of sand burning like sleet.

The plowman jilted her—pulled up roots,
ran off to greener pastures.

Smothered like one of those ashen ladies
of the night of Pompeii
beneath a vast and shifting dune ...

Dug out, now, swept off, fenced in—
made artifact.

Surely a bird-dropped seed of grass
sometimes extends a root.

We picnic upon the bones
of Vikings—in the hundred mouths
of their nearby graves.
Our children clamber
on stones set in childlike imitation

of those treasured ships of theirs,
dragon stem and stern crudely erect.

As we gawk through wire
at the wonder of the field,
hair whipping our faces,
we get a whiff of old sailors
gathering behind us—
sea-smell and mead-fumes:
old sailors whom she has made
to feel alive.

When we leave, it's as if the wind
is taking us.

MOSAIC

No ozone at this height.
Just light, Olympian,
pouring from the cobalt bottle
of Cretan sky,
pouring onto the bleached altar of Lappa.

Rough Guide drew me, scavenging,
to this mountain village,
to the loose fence of chicken wire
around the mosaic floor—
inlaid Madonna too dull, nearly,
to distinguish.

A young man—he is striking—
works the puzzle.
No other life signs,
not even the usual skeletal cat.
"Byzantine?" I smile. Repeat,
again smile.

He does not hear—
no, will not hear.
He refuses to see me.

I stalk the crumbling alley
to an arched doorway
whose massive boards have rotted
a wormhole.
My eye absorbs the glare
of a roofless room
where fissured *pithoi* of Minoan design
flank a worn stone lion—Venetian.
The dust of ruins built

upon ruins. This is no place
for mortals.

In something like snow-blindness,
I face the double axe-head of the sun.

A thick black shape—a widow—
punctuates the white.
Shuffling past with a pail of food
for her son, she levels me
with her stare.
She sees what I am not.

You—feeder of men,
burier of men—only you exist here.
You may shelter your son only so long
before the pattern of his cells
fragments
like the tile in his fading hands—
before, like me,
like your ghost-husband sitting
hunched outside the *kafeneion*,
he is a shell of salt.

SECOND STORY

Plaka, Athens

She watches the day dissolve and dim,
the old woman at the open window.
Her lace blouse falls like a curtain.
Her fat gray cat sleeps on the sill.

From the shadows of the alley below,
a young man appears, his arm around the waist
of a woman in white. Thin legs, gold hair,
the woman looks up, shows her teeth,
speaks American, waves her camera.

The old one pats at her hair.
It sticks like cobwebs to her hands.
She pulls at the neck of her blouse,
sits the cat in front of her like a doll.
They wait for the flash.

The tourists take their laughter with them,
disappear into her son's ouzeri.
Small lights on strings come on in the street.
Rain, uncommon this late in spring, begins to fall.

CEMETERY VENUS

My best friend that killed herself? She had this angel room.
Everything in it was angels.

Spiders can't get enough of you.
They've basted the folds of your gown,
loose-stitched your hair, neck, wings. . . .
Those might be wings teased up
to meet behind your head
or a giant ashtray shell.
You're nine feet tall—
and think you're queen?
Down here, the slabs are grimy-green,
the crosses worn to stumps.
Don't be too proud.
You're concrete from a mold,
rough as the sidewalks that bloodied our knees
when Faye and I were girls
and ran too fast.

A cricket limps across your breast.
Ants crisscross your toes.
Your arms reach; you lean forward
luring souls to your grave heart.
Or is it balance you're after?
A fall would be shattering.
Only a fool would trust you.
Your eyes are a blind person's eyes.
"Who cares?" sign your open palms.
Still, I grab your fingers,
grate them against my own
to get some feeling back.

RESTITUTION: SWALLOWTAILS

The chimenea on my patio,
terra cotta belly atop two three-toed feet,
Neolithic goddess.
I should feed it spicy piñon.
Instead I gut manila files onto the spread of bricks
beneath those elephantine toes.

When the flames set to eating,
Visa statements pleat into small accordions,
curl into pinecones, burst into peonies.
A sigh. The blaze-orange wilts.
All is white and powdery gray
like the end of the world
or the beginning before the creation of color.

I shove in a stack—
all calls to and from my cell phone, ever.
Thick as the Yellow Pages.

Strange how fire makes its own wind.

On what's left of my potted parsley—
from stems they dangle, caterpillars like gravid buds
unfazed by the drifting ashes.
Their mandibles never stop moving.

The caterpillars—I count five—are fat and black
with yellow dots and pale green rings.
They have long rows of gluey mitts.
Last fall I picked them off and killed them.
And when there were no butterflies,
I knew I'd sinned.

Near the end,
the chimenea flames into bloom, dies back.
All proof of my existence—receipts and pay stubs—
a belly of ashes, silky as a cocoon.
Come summer, swallowtails will return
to my lavender and phlox, my pink verbena,
their wings like painted Asian fans,
like flames not yet dying.

ANTS IN AUGUST

On my brick patio
in the middle of morning
a cockroach, lacquered, buzzard-black,
hops on its back like
water flicked on a red-hot griddle,
a Holy Roller in a fit of ecstasy.

Edging closer,
I find it dead—well,
dead enough. (One wing's askew.)
And rivers of ants
tiny as dirt are teasing it apart.
What a frenzy over this Gulliver!
What a tug-of-war over relics!

My bricks picked clean—
a miracle
if not for the imperceptible tremors
of zealots gone underground
to feed in dark earth
their fat blind queen.

HAWKS AND JAYS (1)

Late August downpours
leave bad luck, streets
of shattered mirrors.
Broken asphalt reflects
the edgy shut-down of summer:
clouds on the skids,
the moss-slick underlimbs of oaks,
a stream of birds (a Chinese Dragon Kite),
the moon a pallid dewclaw,
and one hawk shearing the sky's stale blue—
the same hawk maybe that sat itself
in our backyard's Bradford Pear,
full-flowering in May,
and gutted that fat blue jay,
working its talons like crochet hooks.

HAWKS AND JAYS (2)

Nearly October.
Still, heat grips.
Wave after wave, a fall of city rain—
our neighbor's sprinkler.

The hawks won't leave the neighborhood—
the pair that sobbed summer-long
for prey, white throats,
white underwings, slashing
the drought-stricken, strictly blue sky.
Who-we? He-you. Jays chased
the rising, falling, funereal vibrato.

Plagues came:
birdbath water stagnant overnight,
azaleas and twelve-foot viburnums
boiled by whiteflies down to sticks.
Dull shears
snipped the snaking jasmine.
Its sticky milk bled out.

All summer I pictured talons
clamped around panting half-feathered
chicks, their small sharp beaks
unhinged as though for feeding.

THANKSGIVING

Behind our parents' redbrick rancher
where they will live forever,
my brother and I skirt the tree-fringed field
where we as children flew kites.
November sun tilts towards evening,
kindles the chinaberry trees and rolled hay bales,
deepens deer tracks and the churned dirt
of wild hogs rooting.
Steve points through pines to a weed-choked rise,
cemetery abandoned two centuries back,
markers long rotted.
He's into green; he wants to feed the earth.
I comb the sky for buzzards,
spot three, narrowing their orbit.
"A good day to die."
For me, smoke signals, a scattering,
here in our many footprints.

DECORATION

Photograph of a Young Soldier, WWI

They've inverted a soup bowl on his head.
They've bibbed him
for his protection
with his very own gas-mask-in-a-bag.
The square sack hangs crooked
and swollen on his chest.
On his face, a slapped-dumb look.

His country is asking *this*?

Lungs still good, still fresh
off the farm,
he labors to breathe
the frigid air of France,
a stale crust.
Tinned horsemeat to chew—
not what he's used to.

He is ending all wars.
Well, all right.

In the ashen print
my grandfather's blue eyes
wear coins of white light;
his fingernails glow.

Now, years after his early death
(pneumonia in mustard-burnt lungs),
the gas mask hangs
like a chrysalis
or the mask of an alien

from an early horror film
in my paneled den.

AFTER THE FUNERAL, INTO THE SWAMP

The scent of wild lilies rises.
Knowing where they hide, I go down
through wild grape and pokeberry, down
to the pond's black edge-mud. There
in almost no sunlight,
white star-shapes that smell . . . why, heavenly.
I pluck a handful, bury my face.

My grandfather's arms lift me
and my sap-dripping lilies high
above the briers and muck,
onto his shoulders.
Pollen streaks my fingers. I taste,
expecting the sweet yellow of honey,
the dry no-taste of dust.

ONE PHOTOGRAPH SPARED

Nellie Rogers Mace, 1895-1940

Back turned, arms akimbo, she stirs.
Wooden spoon, cast-iron pot, coal-fed stove.
At her waist, the bow of an apron loosening.
Her dress, flower-strewn calico.
She has no face, my father's mother . . .
No hand—no script, looped cursive
or grease-spattered print—to lift
to my tongue what simmers:
field peas? stewed tomatoes? scuppernongs for jam?
Through a window the late-morning sun
catches a braid twisted up off her neck.

Hard times. But come noon
she never turned one soul away—
not even Uncle Frank, who chewed his pork chop
real good then fed it to me like a bird
when I was a chap, perched on the table.

Seven years dying, she hammers into him
faith in that Better Place awaiting her,
till at last in a fancy box in the parlor,
smiling the smile he's come near to forgetting,
she's clearly *there.*
Eleven, my father runs rings around her,
whoops like a Saturday Matinee Indian.
Beneath his black hat, Uncle Frank frowns.

It must be the kitchen—all relatives gone
and Mother in the ground—that stops him cold.
The kitchen stale and still.
He gathers what's left of her—

photographs, the length of auburn hair
cut for her final struggle.
He gathers himself as well—all the pictures
he can find of the child whose ringlets
his father forced her to shear
for school and the world to come.

In the kitchen garden
east of the scuppernong arbor,
he lays a fire, stirs with a stick.
Thyme and sage season the smoke that rises.

THE FEAST OF SNAILS

The artist Alice Lok Cahana, who speaks this poem, survived Auschwitz and Bergen-Belsen. Her sister Edith did not survive the Holocaust.

1

CHILDRENS' CONTEST. AUSCHWITZ, DECEMBER 1944

For turning our barracks festive,
we have nothing.
A broom in a corner.
What good is a broom?
Unbound, it splinters into gold.
We raise, each girl, one broomstraw—
stand, as trained, to attention,
our heights rising towards Edith.
Use what you have, the guards said,
then saw us create
a candelabrum of children.

2

THE PRIZE

I tell them anyway—
my mother, my baby brother,
my tall grandfather,
to whom everyone once bowed:
we won! with—you'll never guess—
a menorah!
The guards said this
is Christmas, then gave us tins

of snails. Edith says to wait—
a banquet of snails on my birthday!

3

TO BERGEN-BELSEN

Snow flies like sparks
into our faces. In others' shoes—
they eat through blisters—
we walk for days.
Our minds scatter like straw.
In such weather, legs splinter.
The tall evergreens watch.
I pity them—their shroud
of frozen tears.

4

DEATH MARCH

"Thank you, but I am not hungry"—
I smirked behind wavering candles.
Hands in lap, my fingers creased
the starched napkin. Mother frowned.

She came to my bed. "Here, drink."
Warm cocoa in cut glass. "You shame me,
you are so thin. My friends think
I'm a bad mother. Drink."

We rake with finger-bones at snow.
Like sheep, we gnaw the little green beneath.

Edith whispers: "Today, Alice."
I'm 16. We eat the German snails.

THE GARDEN OF THE FUGITIVES

Pompeii

They never reached the Nuceria Gate.
Last prayers sputtered out here
with this mime show, shapes blind as grubs
inside a glass mausoleum.
Doomed to try not to die, the Ash People
hold out for ruah, a magic kiss, resurrection.
Why not? Living things are drawn to them.
A snail follows the arc of a small child's skull.
A lizard stalks a mother's back.
Birdlime streaks the arm of a man
who never stopped pulling himself to his feet.
I breathe into the glass.
Nearby a vineyard: the whining of bees
reminds me of home.

Eight hours I've wandered this ghost town.
The dust of the dead plasters
my sweat to my skin.
Where are they?
A last-minute tourist is out of breath.
I nod. He aims his Pentax.
Poor souls, we are no saviors.
At the horizon, a bruise-purple lump:
Vesuvius breathing?
Or the sighing of dust in the vines? . . .

Summers in Louisiana,
cicadas sing themselves out of body,
slit their own backs, escape with wings of glass.
Come morning, brown shells, common curiosities,
cling to cannas, tree trunks, blades of liriope.

Like Hansel's crumbs they litter the sidewalk—
as if there were a prayer for a way home.